St. Mary Catholic School
210 Gurler Road
DeKalb, Illinois
60115

BLAZERS

MILITARY VEHICLES

★ ★ ★ ★ ★ ★ ★ ★ ★ ★ ★ ★ ★ ★ ★

U.S.
ARMY
TANKS

by Carrie A. Braulick

★ ★ ★ ★ ★ ★ ★ ★ ★ ★ ★ ★ ★ ★ ★

Reading Consultant:
Barbara J. Fox
Reading Specialist
North Carolina State University

Capstone
press
Mankato, Minnesota

Blazers is published by Capstone Press,
151 Good Counsel Drive, P.O. Box 669, Mankato, Minnesota 56002.
www.capstonepress.com

Library of Congress Cataloging-in-Publication Data
Braulick, Carrie A., 1975–
    U.S. Army tanks / by Carrie A. Braulick.
    p. cm.—(Blazers—military vehicles)
    Includes bibliographical references and index.
    Summary: "Provides an overview of the design, uses, weapons, and
equipment of U.S. Army tanks"—Provided by publisher.
    ISBN-13: 978-0-7368-5469-6 (hardcover)
    ISBN-10: 0-7368-5469-X (hardcover)
    1. Tanks (Military science)—United States—Juvenile literature. 2. United
States. Army—Equipment and supplies—Juvenile literature. I. Title. II. Series.
UG446.5.B68345 2006
623.7'4752'0973—dc22   2005016447

Editorial Credits
Mandy Marx, editor; Thomas Emery, designer; Jo Miller, photo researcher/
    photo editor

Photo Credits
AP Wide World Photos/Adam Butler, 27
Corbis/ George Hall, 4–5; Leif Skoogfors, 24–25; Reuters, 15, 26;
    USMC/SSgt Jonathan C. Knauth, 6
DVIC, 8–9; JO2 (SW) Stacy Young, 13; Paul Thomas, 7
Folio Inc., 19 (bottom), 28–29
Photo by Ted Carlson/Fotodynamics, cover, 11(both), 14, 19 (top), 20,
    22–23
Photo courtesy of General Dynamics Land Systems, 16–17
UNICORN Stock Photos/Chris Boylan, 12

1 2 3 4 5 6 11 10 09 08 07 06

TABLE OF CONTENTS

Army Tanks

The last thing enemies want to
see is a U.S. Army tank rumbling at
them. Just one blast from the tank's
main gun turns a target into rubble.

The U.S. Army has the world's best tanks. For about 80 years, these powerful machines have shown their strength on battlefields.

BLAZER FACT

During World War II
(1939–1945), fake tanks
were used on battlefields
to fool enemies.

DESIGN

The U.S. Army uses Abrams tanks. These tanks are short and wide. Their low height makes them harder for enemies to hit.

Tanks have layers of strong
metal armor. The armor keeps
the crew safe from enemy attacks.

ARMOR

ROAD WHEEL

TRACK

Two large tracks push tanks over
even the roughest land. The tracks wrap
around road wheels. A large engine spins
the road wheels to make the tracks turn.

BLAZER FACT

Some people call the M1A1 the "whispering death" because its engine is so quiet.

Fully loaded, Army tanks weigh
more than 10 elephants. But they can
still move quickly. Tanks can travel up
to 45 miles (72 kilometers) per hour.

BLAZER FACT

Abrams tanks are the fastest tanks in the world. But even at its highest speed, its guns fire accurately.

★ ★ ★ ★ ★

M1A1 ABRAMS TANK

WEAPONS AND EQUIPMENT

The spinning turret on top of a tank holds its most deadly weapon. The main gun can destroy targets up to 2 miles (3.2 kilometers) away.

TURRET

MAIN GUN

Tanks also have three smaller guns. These machine guns are used for close range combat. They fire at targets nearby.

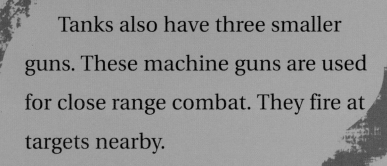

BLAZER FACT

Bullets from the main gun travel faster than 1 mile (1.6 kilometers) per second.

PERISCOPE

Crew members look through sights and periscopes to see outside. Thermal sights sense heat from objects. Crews use thermal sights to spot enemies at night.

MAIN GUN

ROAD WHEEL

MACHINE GUNS

TURRET

TRACK

ARMY TANKS ON DUTY

Tank crews are made up of four people. The driver steers the tank. The gunner and loader run the main gun. The commander leads the crew.

Tanks work in groups to protect each other. Working together helps crews make their missions successful.

BLAZER FACT

Tanks usually work in groups of four called platoons.

RUMBLING ONWARD

GLOSSARY

armor (AR-mur)—a protective metal covering

machine gun (muh-SHEEN GUN)—a large gun that fires bullets quickly

main gun (MAYN GUN)—a tank's largest gun

periscope (PER-uh-skope)—a viewing device with mirrors at each end; tank crew members use periscopes to view their surroundings.

road wheel (ROHD WEEL)—a large, heavy wheel that connects the track to the tank

sight (SITE)—a viewing device in a tank; crew members use sights to aim at targets.

target (TAR-git)—something that is aimed or shot at

track (TRAK)—a flat, rubber belt that connects to a tank's road wheels; tanks travel on tracks.

READ MORE

Gibbs, Lynne. *Tanks.* Mega Books. North Mankato, Minn.: Chrysalis Education, 2003.

Green, Michael, and Gladys Green. *Main Battle Tanks: The M1A1 Abrams.* War Machines. Mankato, Minn.: Capstone Press, 2004.

Zuehlke, Jeffrey. *Tanks.* Pull Ahead Books. Minneapolis: Lerner, 2006.

INTERNET SITES

FactHound offers a safe, fun way to find Internet sites related to this book. All of the sites on FactHound have been researched by our staff.

Here's how:

1. Visit *www.facthound.com*
2. Type in this special code **073685469X** for age-appropriate sites. Or enter a search word related to this book for a more general search.
3. Click on the **Fetch It** button.

FactHound will fetch the best sites for you!

INDEX